Managing Endowment Income

The Moorgate Model for Managing Endowment Distributions

Douglass William List, CFA

MOORE-GATE.

Charlcote Publishing, LLC
1500 Union Avenue, Suite 1310
Baltimore, MD   21211

Introduction

How to manage distributions from the endowment?
This question is probably the most frequent - and often
seemingly intractable - corporate finance problem
faced by non-profit boards everywhere.

- How do we balance short-term cash
  needs against protecting the long-term
  health of the endowment?

- How can we make reasonable
  judgements on how much to withdraw
  each year when the value of the
  endowment itself is constantly moving
  up and down?

- How can we avoid spending so much
  time revisiting this question over and
  over and over again as different players
  come and go with different opinions as
  to what is the appropriate level of
  endowment distributions?

In short, *how can we manage our endowment in a way that
it adds to our financial stability, rather than becoming yet
another source of financial uncertainly?*

Most organizations feel compelled to invest their endowment in the stock market (and other similar assets) in pursuit of higher long-term returns. With these higher returns, however, comes higher variability in the value of the endowment over time. With the value of the endowment going up and down, how do we know whether or not we are taking too much out of the endowment to meet current needs for income? How can we keep swings in market value from playing havoc with our annual budget as down markets create pressure to reduce distributions when we most need them while up markets tempt us to spend beyond our long-term means?

In this note, we will look at several different approaches to managing distributions from endowments. We will review how conventional models focused on the distribution *rate* (distributions as a percentage of endowment assets) produce distribution patterns that aren't all that helpful to stabilizing the finances of the endowment owner - and don't really protect distributions against major disruptions in stock market values. And we will see how a different approach - one that focusses on creating a stable stream of predictable distribution *payments* within the constraints imposed by investing in the stock market - can transform an endowment from being a constant source of anxiety into a solid year after year contributor to the financial health of its owner.

Traditional Distribution Models

Traditional approaches to managing endowment distributions fall into two broad categories that we will refer to as the *specific income* model and the *sustainable distribution rate* model.

Specific Income Model

Years ago, the specific income model was almost universal. Investment portfolios were principally comprised of bonds which paid fixed rates of interest. Bond interest payments were considered income for distribution purposes, and all such income was distributed each year to the endowment owner. As financial markets became more sophisticated and returns from bonds fell as bond risks decreased, stocks were increasingly added to the mix, and stock dividends were included with interest payments on bonds in computing income available for distribution. But even with the initial addition of stocks to the asset mix, we still had a beautifully simple model to follow - income was income and the assets were the assets. Income was distributed, the assets were not.

Not only were distributions easy to determine, they also tended to be highly predictable and stable from year to year, at least in the short term. While the trading values of stocks and bonds go up and down in the market over time, the dividends and interest they pay are usually either constant (interest payments) or gradually increasing (dividends) over time. If the asset base was essentially held constant, "income" levels were very predictable from year to year even as the market value of the asset portfolio rose and fell. And cash receipts and income earned were essentially the same. Whatever the endowment "earned" was received in cash and that cash was distributed to the owner of the endowment.

The specific income model essentially fell apart, however, when dividends ceased to be the primary means by which companies rewarded their shareholders. More and more companies lowered or even discontinued dividends, holding the cash internally to grow the business. The shareholder was expected to cash out by selling the stock rather than by collecting dividends over time. The arguments for the change were compelling - tax reduction and/or deferral for the shareholder, more shareholder control over income timing, lower financial pressures on the operation of the business, and avoided costs in raising cash to grow the business. But the change greatly complicated the problem of managing distributions from investment portfolios such as endowments.

Rather than being comprised primarily of interest and dividend payments, investment income relevant to distributions now had to be expanded to incorporate a third category of income - gains (and losses) on the value of the asset portfolio itself - the extent to which the market value of the underlying assets increased or decreased over a specific period of time. These gains and losses were further divided into *unrealized* (the assets haven't changed, just what they are worth) and *realized* (the assets were sold at either a cash profit or a cash loss). While this change was appropriate as it better reflected economic reality, the congruence between cash received and income earned was destroyed. All asset sales produce cash available for distribution, usually much in excess of the income earned (or lost) on the sale. How are we now to decide what portion of the cash available inside the endowment should be distributed versus that portion which should be reinvested in other assets to protect the long term value of the endowment? Should we in fact sell assets for the specific purpose of making more funds available for distribution?

Total Return

The trend for companies to pay lower and lower dividends to their shareholders eventually resulted in widespread adoption of the *total return* approach to assessing investment portfolio performance. This approach implicitly recognizes that proceeds from the sale of securities will now be available for use as an ongoing source of cash for distributions rather than simply a source of funds for purchasing replacement assets. There are, however, two serious problems with managing distributions in the context of the total return approach:

1. From year to year, the total return on a portfolio can vary dramatically - it can in fact be negative; and

2. While it is very easy to calculate an historic total return for a portfolio, it is essentially impossible to predict the future total return with any certainty, especially in the short run.

The variability in total return from year to year makes total return essentially useless in managing distributions. We can't match income to distributions. If we did, distributions would change dramatically from year to year, and in some years losses would require negative distributions - transfers of funds *into* the endowment!

Nor, as the famous ever-repeated footnote explains, can we blindly rely on past results to predict future performance. It can take a very long time to discover the long term average return from a portfolio. There is an element of common sense to the idea that if we look back five years and compute an average, we should be able to use that average as an estimate for the five years ahead. Eminently sensible. But that is not the way investment returns work in the real world.

Thus, in a world that measures itself on the basis of total returns, we have lost both of our key fixed points of reference for managing distributions. We have lost the clear congruence of income equals cash received equals appropriate distribution, and we have lost the constancy between the income produced last year and the income we can expect to earn this year.

Sustainable Distribution Rate Models

To manage a portfolio *prospectively* under the total return model, someone, often an investment manager with input from an investment committee of some sort, must estimate the *reasonable long-term expected return* from the portfolio, incorporating not only dividends and interest but also returns to be generated from appreciation in the value of the underlying assets, realized over time in part from sales of those assets. Based upon this estimate of the future long-term return of the portfolio, another estimate is produced, that of the *reasonable long-term sustainable distribution rate* that should be used in determining distributions from the portfolio. This later number may be the same as the first, but it is often a little bit lower - injecting a bit of conservatism into a process that is anything but precise.

While this approach represents a logical response to a real problem, it relies heavily on the judgement of the parties involved. Setting a reasonable distribution rate under this framework is at best an imprecise science. At worst, it is a open invitation to give wishful thinking a seat at the table, stretching the definition of reasonable based upon the asserted needs of the moment. There is no way to determine the correctness of the estimate until enough history has passed to make the assessment of correctness largely irrelevant. In particular, by the time it is clear that the rate was set too high, it is usually painfully obvious that recovering from the error will be, well, painful.

Focussing on an estimated sustainable distribution rate is attractive in part because lay people feel comfortable discussing such an assumption. They can compare it to the interest rate on their mortgage and to the return assumptions being used by the planner helping them with retirement planning. It is sometimes amazing to hear the spirited discussion around the boardroom about what is reasonable based on the rather dubiously relevant personal experiences of those in the room. (Most estimated sustainable distribution rates tend to fall within a range between 4% and 6%.) But the real policy decision that matters most relates to how the estimated rate is to be *used,* not its precise value.

The biggest problem with focusing on a sustainable distribution *rate* is that, if used to compute distributions on an annual basis, the resulting distributions will go up and down with the underlying

changes in the value of the investment portfolio -
sometimes dramatically. In Figure 1, we can see the
highly volatile distributions that would have resulted
from using a fixed 4.5% annual distribution rate on a
model portfolio. (The model portfolio we use in this
illustration - and those that follow - tracks the
management of $100,000 invested in the S&P 500 at the
beginning of 1951. As is typical with such illustrations,
we assume a tax-free environment, and no transaction
or management costs in assessing various distribution
management strategies.)

Note that over the 63 years covered by this chart, in 22
years (shown in red) the endowment owner would
have experienced a decline in endowment distributions
under a model where distributions are set at 4.5% of
assets. Invariably, organizations that attempt to adhere
to a reasonable fixed distribution rate find themselves
compelled to revisit distribution policies frequently to
deal with the unpleasant side of this volatility. (The
down years are the bummers. Everyone loves to boast
about the up years!)

Rolling Specified Distribution Rate

A common response to the volatility experienced with
a fixed distribution rate is to attempt to smooth
distributions by using some sort of a rolling average
that incorporates several years of historic portfolio
value in setting distributions. In Figure 2, we model
one such approach by applying a 4.5% distribution rate
to the rolling three-year average value of the
underlying portfolio, one of the more popular
smoothing techniques in use today.

Surprisingly enough, under the rolling three-year
average model, we see only a modest improvement in
terms of the number of years in which the distribution

declines. We do, however see something of a reduction in the severity of the changes from year to year. So this approach is indeed somewhat less disruptive than applying a fixed percentage on an annual basis, but it still doesn't look particularly attractive.

We could experiment with different long term averages, and indeed could certainly reduce the magnitude of the swings, but even with very long averages, distributions will rise and fall as down years fall out of the average and then re-enter. Since there is no averaging approach that really works on a sustainable basis, the end result is inevitably a long and usually difficult board meeting where once again the distribution policy must be revised to deal with the reality of the old policy not meeting the demands of the day.

Is there a better way we might proceed?

FIGURE 1

DISTRIBUTIONS AT 4.5% OF ENDOWMENT VALUE

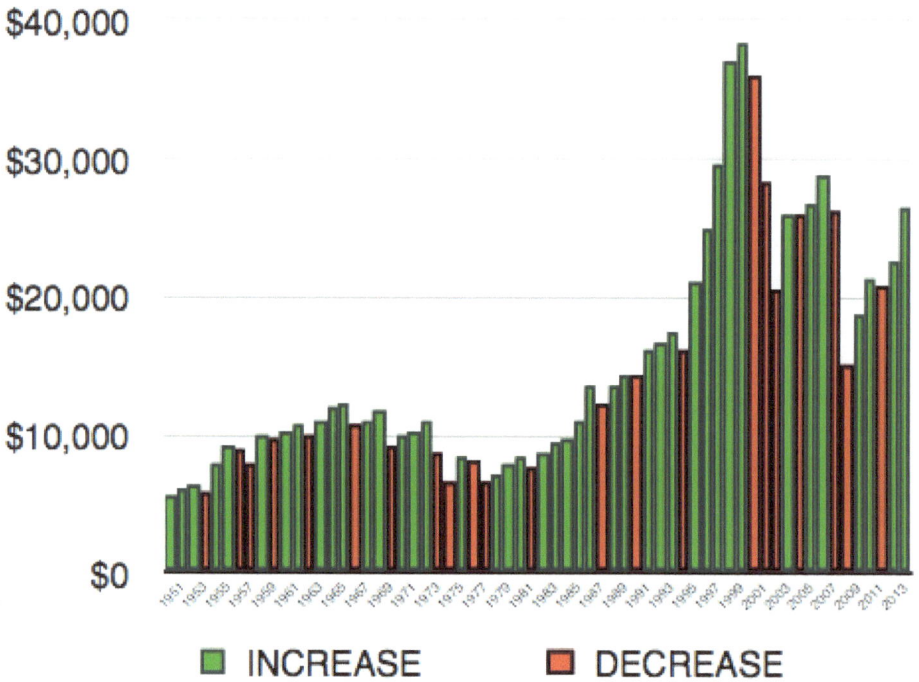

FIGURE 2

DISTRIBUTIONS AT 4.5% OF THREE YEAR TRAILING AVERAGE OF ENDOWMENT VALUE

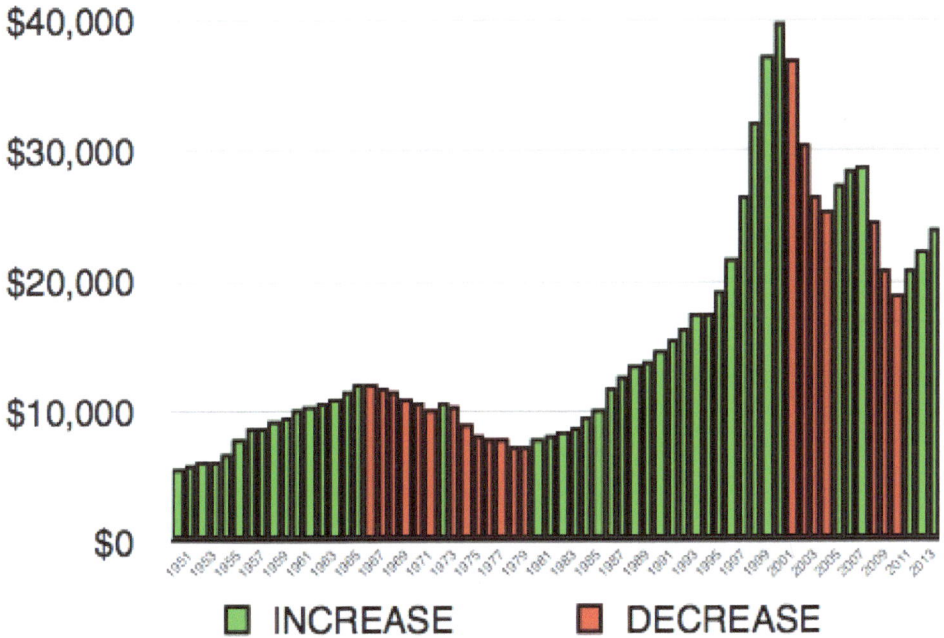

■ INCREASE   ■ DECREASE

Moorgate's Ratchet Distribution Model

The critical first step to a better model is to look at the problem from a different point of view. In developing an effective distribution strategy, **we should start not with the dynamics of the endowment, but with the needs of the organization that owns the endowment**. The organization is most concerned in the short-run with the distribution *amount*, not the distribution *rate*. If we take the perspective of the endowment owner, we find ourselves longing for the good old days - stable, predictable income. Something we can count on when everything else seems unstable. The Moorgate Ratchet Distribution Model was created from this perspective.

The Moorgate ratchet model starts with the assumption that, from the perspective of the owner, an ideal distribution model would have three primary attributes:

1. The distribution model will not threaten the long term health of the endowment.

2. Distributions will rarely if ever decline from year to year, making them a highly reliable source of funding annual operations.

3. In the long-term, distributions will increase in a meaningful way.

To meet these criteria, we need to accept a lower *average* distribution rate while we set our focus on managing the distribution itself, rather than the distribution rate. In doing so, we can create a distribution environment consistent with the rational objectives of the owner.

1. We can maintain a stable distribution amount without jeopardizing the long-term health of the underlying investment portfolio;

2. We can promote the long-term growth rate of the investment portfolio; which in turn means that

3. We can enhance the long-term impact of the endowment on the operations and financial strength of the owner.

Three Basic Parameters

The Moorgate ratchet model requires that we set three basic parameters to govern the calculation of annual distributions:

1. **A target distribution rate**. This rate sets the default level of distributions from the endowment when no other constraint applies. In the examples that follow, we will set this rate at 3%.

2. **A maximum allowable distribution rate**. This is the absolute upper bound on the distribution rate, set to protect the portfolio from destructive levels of distributions in the event of a major decline in asset values. In the examples that follow, we use 6% as the

maximum distribution rate that we will accept. (The 2:1 relationship of 6% to 3% is deliberate, as it exceeds the top to bottom value ratios of major market declines.)

3. **A distribution acceleration limit**. This is the maximum percentage by which we will allow the distribution amount to increase from year to year. Dramatic declines in investment values are usually preceded by periods where asset prices increase at rates that are not sustainable. To reduce our vulnerability to future market declines, we cap the rate at which the distribution amount can increase during up markets regardless of how fast the value of the portfolio may be increasing. In our example we will set this limit at 10%.

A distribution policy reflecting the parameters laid out above might read as follows:

> *The distribution from the endowment for the current year shall be calculated as the **higher** of 3% of the value of the portfolio at the beginning of the year or the amount of the prior year distribution, except that the distribution **cannot exceed either 110%** of the prior year distribution or **6%** of the value of the endowment portfolio at the beginning of the year.*

The Uncapped Ratchet Scenario

To better illustrate how the ratchet model works, we will first apply it *without* the cap on year-to-year increases in distributions.

In Figure 3, we show the distribution pattern that would result from setting the initial distribution at 3%

and then allowing the distribution to ratchet up with the investment portfolio, never falling below a 3% distribution rate. At the same time, when the value of the portfolio falls, the distribution level remains flat so long as the distribution does not exceed 6% of portfolio value. At that point, the distribution amount is reduced to ensure that the 6% rate is not exceeded.

Note that under this scenario, even without the 10% growth cap, distributions to the endowment owner fall in only one year, 2009, following the major market decline in 2008. The three year market decline that begins in 2001 results in distributions going flat, but not decreasing.

Ratchet Scenario with 10% Cap

In Figure 4, we see the impact of setting a 10% year over year growth cap on distributions. With the growth cap in place, distributions are still increasing in 2001 when the market downturn occurs, and keeping the distribution flat again does not violate the 6% maximum distribution rate boundary. But distributions max out at a lower level than in the previous example due to the capped growth rate. Portfolio growth has just reached the distribution rate down to the three percent minimum threshold when the 2009 downturn begins. Thus, in the income growth capped scenario, the 2009 fall in portfolio value fails to trip the 6% maximum distribution limit. In both major market downturns, the capped ratchet model results in no change to distribution levels at times when endowment owners would likely be under financial stress from other aspects of their operations.

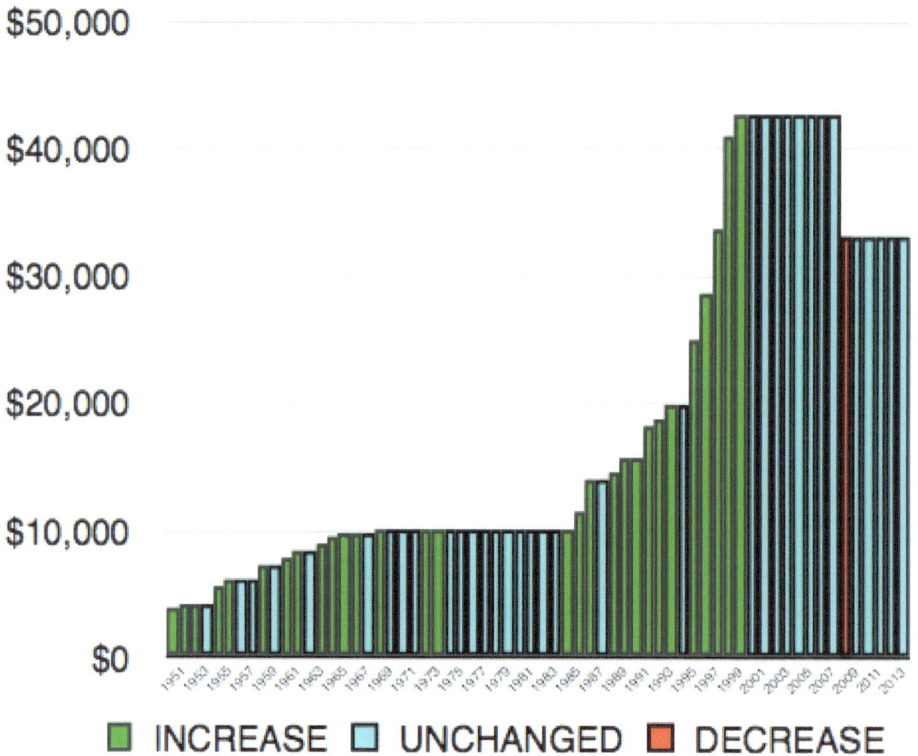

FIGURE 3

RATCHET MODEL MINIMUM 3% MAXIMUM 6% NO CAP ON ANNUAL DISTRIBUTION GROWTH

INCREASE   UNCHANGED   DECREASE

FIGURE 4

RATCHET MODEL MINIMUM 3% MAXIMUM 6%
10% CAP ON ANNUAL DISTRIBUTION GROWTH

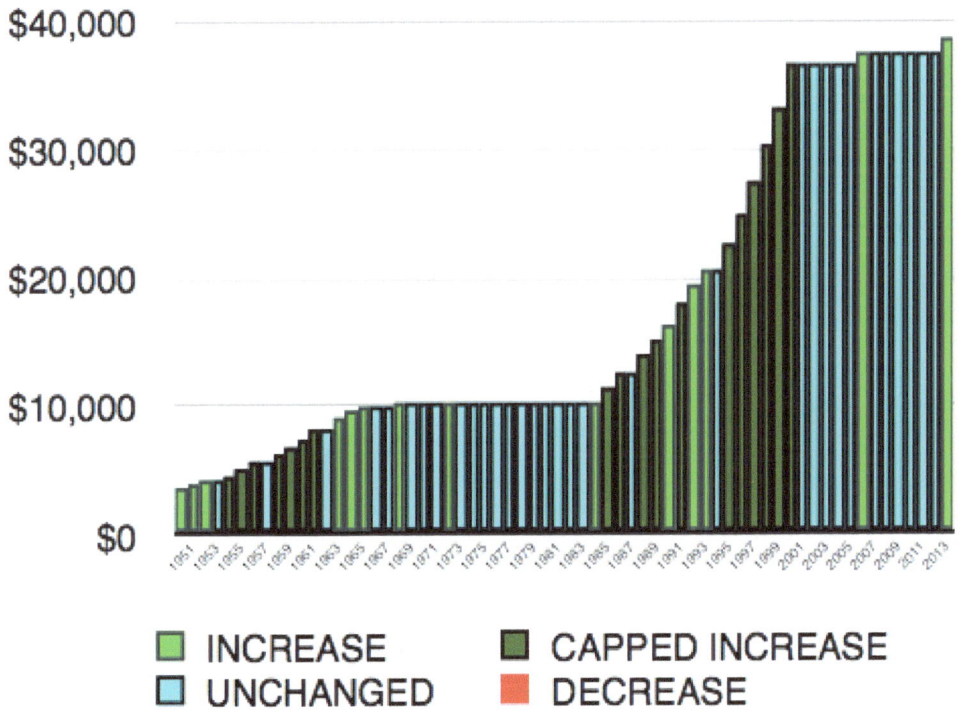

INCREASE   CAPPED INCREASE
UNCHANGED   DECREASE

Comparing the Four Scenarios

As a recap to the discussion above, we can look at how all four approaches fared on a number of metrics.

We can see how the 3/6/10 ratchet strategy dominates the others so long one is willing to accept lower initial distributions in order to "prime the pump." We can see in Figure 5 how under this specific comparison it takes eighteen years for the ratchet strategy to yield the same distribution amount as following the 4.5% basic strategy. However, from that point forward the ratchet model is clearly the dominant strategy. This dominance comes from the fact that the ratchet model strategy is by that time supported by a much stronger investment base, as shown in Figure 6.

TABLE OF COMPARISONS

	DISTRIBUTION STRATEGY			
	Straight 4.5%	**Three Year 4.5%**	**3/6 Ratchet without cap**	**3/6 Ratchet with cap**
Initial Portfolio Value	$100,000	$100,000	$100,000	$100,000
Investment Portfolio	S&P 500	S&P 500	S&P 500	S&P 500
Time Period	1951-2013	1951-2013	1951-2013	1951-2013
Ending Portfolio Value	$564,173	$582,861	$1,068,468	$1,252,892
Total Distributions	$961,187	$974,025	$1,172,441	$1,120,109
Initial Distribution	$5,717	$5,717	$3,811	$3,811
Ending Distribution	$26,584	$24,004	$33,033	$38,749
Ending Distribution / Initial Distribution	465%	420%	867%	1017%
Growth Rate	2.5%	2.3%	3.5%	3.8%
Down Years	22	20	1	0
Worst Decline	42.8%	17.5%	22.8%	N/A

FIGURE 5

COMPARISON OF ANNUAL DISTRIBUTIONS
4.5% BASIC MODEL VS 3 / 6 / 10 RATCHET MODEL

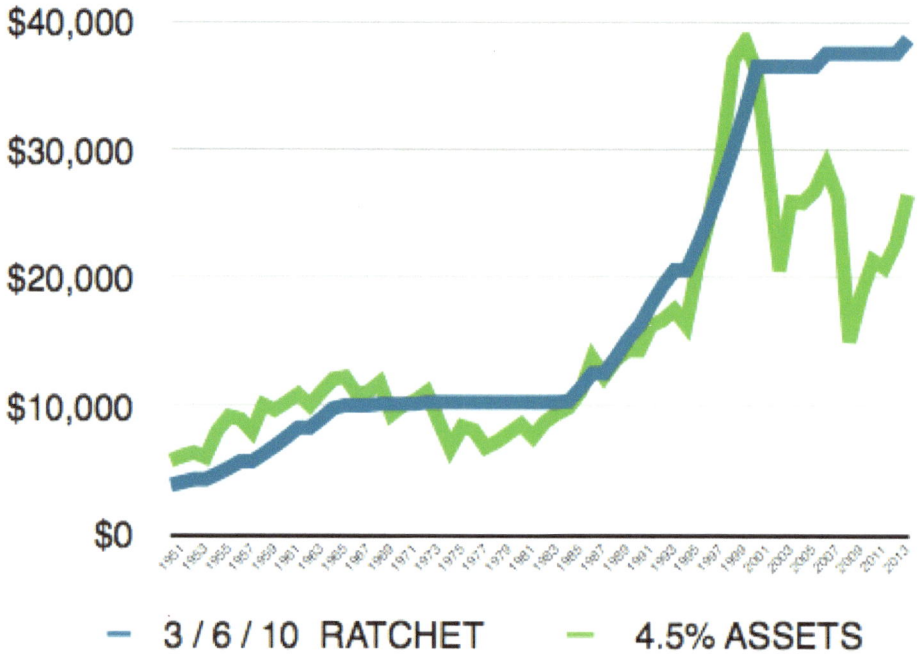

Legend: — 3 / 6 / 10 RATCHET   — 4.5% ASSETS

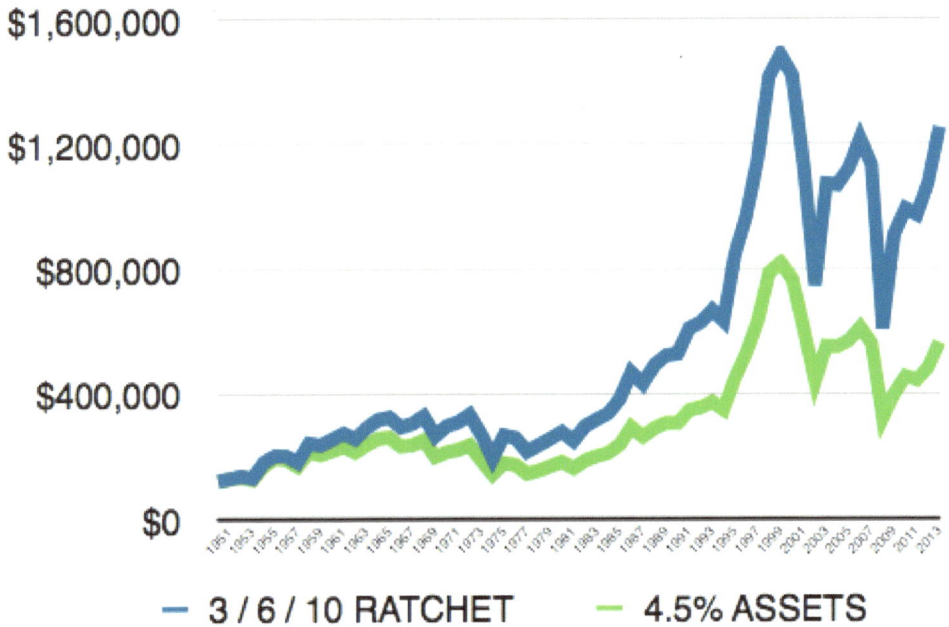

FIGURE 6

COMPARISON OF ENDOWMENT ASSETS
4.5% BASIC MODEL VS 3 / 6 / 10 RATCHET MODEL

— 3 / 6 / 10 RATCHET   — 4.5% ASSETS

Conclusion

The Moorgate Ratchet Distribution Model approach to managing distributions from an endowment offers a very attractive framework for managing distributions in a manner that provides both short-term financial stability to the endowment owner as well as long-term growth in distributions, all without the need to empower portfolio managers to make ad hoc adjustments to a distribution rate based strategy that would be necessary in order to achieve comparable stability and growth in levels of current distributions.

Discussion with the Author

Q: This sounds like an interesting approach. Is anyone using it?

> *A: Yes. The idea was originally developed for the Virginia Glee Club, which uses this approach in managing distributions from its endowment. The Glee Club's endowment portfolio is professionally managed by the University of Virginia Investment Management Company (UVIMCO), but the Glee Club has considerable latitude in setting distributions. The volatility of the UVIMCO portfolio is somewhat lower than that of the S&P 500, but given the longer investment history of the S&P 500, that index was used as a portfolio surrogate for analytical purposes in establishing the distribution policy. .*

Q: Was there a particular motivation for adopting the plan?

> *A. Yes. Three circumstances drove the decision:*
>
> > - *The Glee Club had recently undertaken a major capital campaign that more than doubled the size of its endowment, so there was an understandable interest in revisiting the endowment distribution policy (which until that time had been very ad hoc).*

- *Following the campaign, income from the endowment would represent 30-50% of the Glee Club's income - becoming a key element of the Club's annual budget.*

- *Like other schools, Virginia had just gone through major dislocations resulting from investment losses during the 2008 market decline that triggered forced reductions in endowment distributions which in turn led to forced reductions in staff. The Glee Club recognized that it did not want to be vulnerable to a similar experience at any point in the future.*

  Consequently, the Glee Club was very open to the idea deferring significant increases in current endowment distributions in order to implement a distribution management model that would insulate the Club from unplanned decreases in endowment distributions.

Q: Is there anything special about using the figures of 3%, 6%, and 10% in the model? What about using other assumptions to drive the model?

  A. *One can certainly use other numbers in constructing a strategy using the model. Researchers who have studied the investment universe have concluded that long term pre-tax returns (after inflation) on the order of 5% to 8% are likely to be sustainable. So 3% is well under the expected long-term return and will thus practically guarantee growth in distributions over time. By allowing withdrawals of up to 6% as compared to our basic rate of 3%, we are reasonably protected* against severe declines in current portfolio valuation. If we cap distribution growth at a rate of up to 10%, we can be reasonably sure that portfolio growth won't wildly outrun distribution growth while also being confident that distributions won't chase a runaway bull market. The further one goes above 10% year over year growth, the greater the risk that a future downturn will require a reduction in distributions to protect the financial integrity of the endowment. When investment returns are repeatedly in double digits, all advisors know that current results are unsustainable. What no one knows, however, is when the party will end. When these growth waves occur, an endowment owner wants to follow them, not ride them.

Q: What would be the arguments against using this model?

A. Arguing against this model is essentially arguing for current consumption over greater savings. That's an argument as old as economics. The endowment is the endowment. It will generate some return on whatever assets are there. Do we want to spend more now or have more for later? Or, more to the point, do we want to have more for later _and_ more to protect against unpredictable market declines. We all know how effective people can be when arguing for current consumption over savings. But if you've lived long enough, you are also keenly aware of how important it is to have adequate resources to survive periods of intense financial stress.

Q: How would implementation work in the case of an existing endowment? Would the owner need to lower endowment distributions in order to implement the Moorgate model?

> A. No. *You can start the model as if it was already in place. If your current year distribution of, say, $450,000 represented 4.5% of an endowment of $10,000,000, you can simply freeze the distribution at $450,000 until the endowment grows to $15,000,000, at which time $450,000 would be 3.0% of the endowment and would start to grow with the growth of the endowment. You would need to reduce the withdrawal amount only if the value of the endowment fell 25% to $7,500,000, at which point $450,000 would represent a 6.0% withdrawal rate. It is worth noting, however, that a 25% one year decline in portfolio value is a very plausible occurrence. The sooner one can get the base level of withdrawal down closer to 3.0%, the sooner one gets to a place where the protection against market downturns is very robust.*

Q: How might our current endowment investment advisor react to this concept?

> A. *Any advisor should be able to confirm that this approach will produce results along the lines of those presented. There may be some pushback that the model is too "conservative," depriving the owner of the opportunity to take more money out of the endowment sooner while still being "responsible." But any advisor would have to agree that taking more money out sooner means taking more risk with respect to future distributions during market downturns and will*

retard the long-term growth of endowment distributions.

Advisors are almost certain to recommend investment strategies more sophisticated than simply investing in the S&P 500. Whether such strategies net of fees are more effective than simply investing in index funds is a topic beyond the scope of this conversation. It is worth noting, however, that a distribution strategy along the lines presented here allows an endowment owner to absorb more volatility in portfolio value than is tolerable under most arrangements in place today, opening up the range of reasonable investment strategies that can be considered.

The highly predictable nature of distributions under this model certainly makes the job of the investment manager easier by giving the same level of distribution predictability to the portfolio manager that it provides to the distribution recipient.

31 MOORGATE
AN INVESTMENT MANAGEMENT ADVISORY

List & Company, Inc.
14 Wall Street, 20th Floor
New York, NY 10005

doug.list@listandcompany.com